BURN BOOK

FELIX BERNSTEIN
Burn Book

NIGHTBOAT BOOKS
NEW YORK

ISBN 978-1-937658-42-7

Design and typesetting by Margaret Tedesco
Text set in Gypha and Proforma
Cover illustration by Toni Simon
Burn photo designed by Christopher Wegman

Cataloging-in-publication data is available
from the Library of Congress

Distributed by University Press of New England
One Court Street
Lebanon, NH 03766
www.upne.com

Nightboat Books
New York
www.nightboat.org

For Gabe

One must consent
to burning, burning
in advance and
immediately, not
one thing, but all
that for us represents
things, so as not to
expose oneself to
burning completely.
All that is not burned
by all of Us, and that
does not make Us
Desperates and Loners,
the Earth will burn.

—Antonin Artaud

BURNS

EMMA

Human nature
is supposed to
exist, subsist,
between the
irreconcilable
dualities of good
and evil, restraint
and decadence,
moralism and
hedonism, reality
and artifice,
substance and
surface, truth
and falsehood.

—Emma Bee Bernstein

Hummingbird

Charles watches from the upper deck
Susan with her Popsicle stick
The peeping zap of desire
On the morning lawn

Middle school splashes
Tangy orange chewed up
Grizzle cakes and
Barney pees sticky
Vanilla

My hairlick catches the
Monstrous eye of the barber

We were free then, slurping Gogurt
Jacking off to our own nudity

We were the world's youngest pedophiles
But clitoral tails tore us apart
Ball sacks covered with marmite

Grandpa fell outside of Dean & DeLuca's

Baby lust concealed by
Central Park shrubbery

Look we're casting a shadow on grandpa's grave

His own Axe deodorant
Makes him horny for

Institutional boy culture

The friends forget 9/11 together

Jerry Springer and Tom Green
Show me their things

HDTV asphyxiates my grandmother

Freedom in corndog land
Catdog suckles down
Cinnamon Toast Crunch and
It's not rape if it happens in a lucid dream

Miss Stone

On the first day of class, Miss Stone passes a large glance at me. This is pre-school. And so each large glance is like a thousand rivers of cinema. And cinema is a disturbing demarcation of the powerful unity of time and space in psychological perception. And I learn this in Room 102.

And the kids are jealously planning a funeral for Maggie Magee: the first girl that I put my fingers into. Martin Luther King was a loving man, was a gentle man. I love putting my finger in girls in the schoolyard. But fingers and touching are for books says Mrs. Iyeni with bug eyes and doody freckles.

It's that type of day, Benjamin thinks.

We are reading *Tales of a Fourth Grade Nothing* when Matthew calls in about the twin towers being struck down, and I go home and watch *Pee Wee's Big Adventure*.

"Allison's a boy!" They pointed. They always pointed at the trans students. I mean the proto-trans ones. I hate schools. Because they are prototransphobic. I want all trans people to be okay. Miss Stone yells, "Quit it, she's just trans, one day you will have a degree writing about trans, and you will feel bad for being such an asshole." There is a mustache growing on Allison's face and I do think that is funny. So am I an asshole?

When Roger does his show-and-tell on his trip to England, my khakis rise up and make a hill. "What is that?" asks Lucy.

Noah's house has the TV on all the time. And they drink Diet Pepsi.

Dameon Waloosh was so dishonest his nose grew.

We all love this class rat, Milly, even though he makes Jewls sneeze,
I wanted to name him Tootsie Bacon.

Mac, who has a crush on Kathy, bashed in Tootsie's face.

Allison's mustache is today's lunch topic. She is avoiding the kids,
doing some weird polka thing.

Miss Stone shouted, go to the board, and organize the days of the week.
Jewls' hand stopped with nervousness, as she dropped the Velcro
covered Monday to the ground, and grabbed Tuesday.

"Excellent student ... has issues with peers." Her father sits on the corner
of her bed and tears up her report card. The next day he packs her a
special magic pencil and a sandwich. Daddy's magic pencil makes it
better. It comes with a tiny note: "Writing is a world for your self only."
She smiles, as slowly the school disappears.

Eating the sandwich, Allison tries to think of her future, she secretly
tries to buy a razor, but her mother is freaked out.

My best friend's apartment smells like Kraft macaroni and cheese and
his parents think I'm a sweet comic God. I could leap into his hamper
and live there like a little troll, watching him bring each girlfriend
over but instead I'll eventually learn to settle for ugly gay partners as
groveling as me.

Miss Stone writes with yellowish-green chalk on the board. Everyone
is in class except Deedee because Deedee is at a funeral cause Deedee's
dad is dead. Deedee shook, she swallowed the whole lunch in one gulp.
Her dad was a firefighter in 9/11. Isa thinks Rudy Giuliani is a hero.
I listen to Liza Minnelli's "New York, New York" and cry. Everyone
hates that Albert Einstein's picture hangs on the door, even though his
tongue is out.

Jewls carves the name Jewls in the desk. Mac and Joy are all dressed up for the cultural dance in the gymnasium. I get to dance with the fat children's author Paula Danziger. She twirls. She is the first fag hag that I meet.

Deedee squirts milk out her nose. "Who wants the rest?"

Mrs. Kidswatter, the German lunch lady, is in a really bad mood today. Because the fourth graders keep leaving garbage under the table and now there are cockroaches. Todd was the first to find them. Benjamin thinks they'd make a good class pet. "He's the worst of the boys in the class." Allison hasn't been in school for a week. "Good," yelled Myron. But Benjamin missed her. Does Benjamin love Allison? Paul sits next to Jewls, she has dribbled spit all over the table.

Someone sticks the post-it note 'birdbrain' onto Jewls' back.

Six girls in the class have pigtails. Dana stands up. She even makes Jewls smile, when she reads her book report: "*My Parents Didn't Steal an Elephant* was a very funny and crazy book by Uriah C. Lasso, a funny author to write such a book. It is a story told by a kid. The kid's parents are in jail because they stole an elephant, except they are innocent. Hey! I just realized something. You know what? You never know the kid's name! I just realized that."

Dana can't hear very well and also has bad ankles. She usually sits in the back. But today, for just one day, she is famous.

Everyone, after class, gets together for Mac's birthday. "Let's play Uno!" Joy and Paul are off to the side. Mac is starting to feel queasy.

Kathy snuggles in closer to him. "I love Uno." "Really?"
Today the class will learn to play the bongos.

Wendy and Casper

Wendy and Casper the Friendly Ghost are attempting to kiss but Casper keeps slipping into Wendy's body. When he is in there, he feels really warm and sticky. Wendy asks Casper to gently slip out so that she doesn't get pregnant but it is too late...almost...but when he pushed her, Casper did not anticipate that he would lose Wendy too. After this, Casper squanders his inheritance, loses faith, and ends up a homeless vagabond roaming the streets. Because he is friendly, he cannot ward off thugs, who love to tease and molest him. In the end, he confines himself to a particularly stinky corner in a dark alley. There he sits to this day, sadly wishing that he could exorcise himself for the only one haunted by Casper was Casper. He finally finds a priest who is able to abolish the ghost, and in doing so, Casper dies, as well. There is no heaven, so Casper and Wendy are not united. They are both gone forever.

Sabby

I buried Sabby
Near a little glowworm
I never buried anyone before
But did take pictures of tree shadows
While I was still young enough to care

That was when I let my back rot
Gave up on the girlish daybreak
Of singing

Maybe I was never meant to be a
Pretty mist
Just a hard-edged prick

Diana Tive

Not swerving around the concrete bed of little girls
But holding them in my puny Jewish arms
That can barely pick up a weight let alone a
Jewish princess

And I can masturbate freely up the hill to climax
While grandpa sleeps in the other room

Puffing sublimes thru droplets of skin Choking out No end in sight Just figures blazing Neck twisted to peep Pillow fighting Some worms crawl thru Impaired dream cycle Picturing golden rushes Of soft Beautiful jaggèd Wooden framed maidens Seized by leisure Ever-delayed, fluttering Hissing and swinging Crunched moonbeam sky Clasping ecstatic doves Soupy fog gently seeps Drowsy boy Rest till O'erflowing Devout boy shaking Moaning shivers 'neath night bell Eating porridge Damp covers Sweet echoes Quivering seals sludge Breaking point of morning Neon electric waters Craggly hills with slimy moss Enter the sunken dreams Can't suppress any of them My sister's corpse appearing each time I jerk Off an eternal Rerunning Cum hitting the TV screen We used to watch TV on together

heart sunk
shot her pistil
grassy dew
maneuvered
land unfolded
vacant ports
peach

444 Mutual Friends

Friend all of dad's friends and students on Facebook, like all of their
statuses, comment on all of their statuses, pledge allegiance to certain
ones, distance yourself from others, trust nobody, make strategic
friendships, put certain people forward, pretend to like the statuses
of idiots who write constantly on Facebook, there is no difference
between pretending to like and liking, become an idiot who writes
constantly on Facebook, become a gay internet artist, secretly plot
a critique slowly in your head against the neoliberal and idiotic
tendencies among yourself and your new Facebook friends, bat your
eyes at all queer theory professors you meet, occasionally challenge
one or two professors for their enclosed canon but don't do anything to
get yourself off the invite list, attempt to remain removed and alienated
from the cliques that form around you, but don't do anything to get
taken off the invite list, slowly mount your critique, and let bits and
pieces out into the world, but don't do anything to get taken off the
invite list, smile and bat your eyes at the rising young Internet stars,
poets, and artists around you, who are truly scum of the earth, talk
to dad about these poets and artists, try and figure out why almost
nobody in the 90s spoke up against the bizarre dull trends in poetry
and art, why the few adults that you care about, who have led you to
realize that queer theory and conceptual poetry and post-conceptual
art are bullshit, why they kept silent, and why the few people who
did something different were never prolific enough to warrant major
attention from the academy, art world, or poetry world; you don't
want to lose friends, you don't want to come off as hostile, no ad
hominem attacks dad says, you're already too polemical, why are you
so polemical, are you trying to merely one-up dad, or are you actually
trying to do something different, to engage in a different way with

the world, are you post-oedipal or is that post-oedipal feeling merely the most oedipal thing you could possibly do. Overthrow the nuclear family and its terms but don't get off the invite list. Deconstruct the enthusiasm of those around you but don't get off the invite list. But say hi to Prof. Gregg at dinner, he'll help connect you to Leo Bersani. Can't I just stay in my room and jerk off, alone, without turning that into some sort of redemptive subcultural status. Please?

When I was little I thought I could happily attend events as long as I subverted them through parody and reference to my anus. I thought I could remain on the invite list and that would be fun because I'd bring filth to supper. I thought that was my only choice: that I had to participate vis-à-vis the signifier, albeit a broken signifier, and that this would be fine, as long as I kept shoving excessively stinky signifieds into the system.

But here I am now with a mound of references, and just an anorexic stick of a referent to manage the landfill of hyper-orgasmic pop-ups of perversity that are begging to be integrated into the dinner table chit-chat: so that Leo Bersani and Samuel Delany can talk about the subversivity of my rectum. But I'd rather just jerk off alone in my room.

Life's not a cabaret. And I'm no longer a cherry bomb.

Coy

The first unreality is the deepest
And only really good boys are
Cover ups for each little
Pit, itsy bitsy
Pendulum.
A feminist raped me. The
Dollhouse slut next to
The raven.
I remember having my toenails painted...
I remember having my toenails crushed...
The household is best kept
Plastic-wrapped
So that nobody will
Spot the dollhouse
Faggot's pretty little
Lies

Vaudeville

For Lorenz Hart

Clovers will rot. An intimacy conjured by the crucial
Sighs and words that surround us. We're not, after all
In this concealment for nothing like all pornos it's a
Family act picking our favorite words to cloak our non-
Sentiments. Not being able to trespass knowledge, the
Marker of infidelity. The
Bridge is left always so unformed. Because
No poet emerges on second thought. Vanessa
Founders on the edge of a shoe. Helen Keller did
Vaudeville too. She'd puppet
What she said too. A grimace was enough. I dropped
Three pounds and called it a day. Plotting, scheming to
Make all my money back. Some words we cherish
Seahorses and seesaws make us forget. They try too
Hard to unearth every last bit of tinsel from her
Shelled out anatomy. False eternities conveyed in
Her lyre. False and utter helplessness in her teardrops
This little girl blue went out to market and stayed there
The piggy went home and hid under the bed. Some say
Locked deep inside her skull, when her green ribbon
Comes untied, we see her actual emotional vomit.
The more mute, the more you are a muse, the more
Fisting required, the happier to see you my dear.
Blanket falls right on cue to wrap him. Right as
Snow hits his face. Bullies make him feel
As if it's like he is no less who he already is. That's
Refreshing. Note well that he confuses prison with
Psychic torment from yellowed privileged
Memory. My head cannot convince
Me otherwise. Disintegration is always playful at

First. The opaque kernel of torment that gullibility
Breeds is always filtered out by the
Precise repression machines bedimmed my
Early onset urge to leer
This
Becomes it.
To
Play forever. That is hell. Where a
Hermeneutics of suspicion becomes
Baseless denial of self. Without
vision, I flop. An agnostic
Peacock glides in and out of jargon
And fails to subsist. Showers of tranquil
Colors finally crown me. And knock
Me down to size. A caffeinated
Phantom
Thumb stuck in his own pie. Always
Grosser than you'd think. The only
Thing left that's undreamt is sleep.
Shuddering at the Shoah.
Apples and honey and macaroni
Craft projects. All visions pang.
And a lonely viper storms into
Shower and relief. Climb into
Bed on top of a sweet plume
No fear in sight, lengthened
Boundary, warding off all
Natal reminders of causality

A collective scream is hard
To turn off, scrambles my
Ceiling. I climb three vines
Shaped like tears and reach
A tarn swarming
As soon as
I catch sight of the tare
In river reflection, I
Seek to unrouse myself
Analytically, loosen up
My winter-bright mind
But there is nothing left
That isn't damp and cold
Italy is worse than I thought
And I can't convince myself
Otherwise. Stifled by low
Mist and gondolas, one
Gets the sense that
Felix, if only, your
Balmy eyes...
It's okay to be rich
In some things and
Empty handed in
Others. A new moon
Slants light on a
Puddle and I'm

The Fingernails

There are moods in which we court suffering, in the hope that here,
at least, we shall find reality, sharp peaks and edges of truth. But it
turns out to be scene-painting and counterfeit. The only thing grief
has taught me, is to know how shallow it is...

— Emerson, "Experience"

The fingernails are medium length
and fingernail beds are blue. The
Cold air cause of melancholy.
Comets above the moon.
Confession of his grief to a friend, a principal cure of melancholy.
Conscience troubled, a cause of despair. The
Contention, brawling, lawsuits, effects. The
Continent or inward causes of melancholy.
Copernicus, his hypothesis of the earth's motion
Crocodile's jealous. The
Cure of melancholy, unlawful, rejected; from God; of head-melancholy; over
all the body; of hypochondriacal melancholy; of love-melancholy;
of jealousy; of despair
Cure of melancholy in himself; or friends. The "V" on the anterior of the neck
and an inverted "V" on the posterior of the neck, consistent with hanging.

EBB

I've thought of a centerpiece to make it stick together.

      The book you mean?

Yeah.... I've thought: communicating with the dead. But that would be too creepy.

      Why? Framing is always a way of killing. So no matter what it'll be creepy.

Okay. But this is also corny.

      So is a lot of this book. So is my death. Hanging in a museum.

Cornball.

      So? Art should always be folly.

I quit analysis because it can't handle the whole sibling thing. Daddy this, daddy that. But you were more important than him.

      I was him.

Right I get it. Your last Facebook status: Emma is Charles.

      That's why I didn't need analysis.

But I do since allegedly I have a melancholic fixation on you. I think you were the greatest and cannot be replaced instead of realizing it's my desire that cannot be replaced, that something in you caused desire, something in the male butt caused desire, and I cannot have that thing again. So I fixate on you as "object," a substitute that is never the cause of my desire but resembles it.

> Yeah whatever but also you are dealing with my melancholic fixation on you, i.e., being haunted. But I'm not an object. Or a lack of object. I'm a ghost. And the ghost is in the machine/ego: we share the same machine.

This hurts me so much that I need tranquilizers.

> But you're tranquilizing yourself good enough by fixating more.... You're distracting from larger and more unconscious feelings. Which is fine. But like I said you'll fall asleep either way. Fixate or not doesn't really make a difference. I fixate and send endless texts all the time. But what is singular about the person and what is lost in them is not related to your own attempts to handle your anxiety and panic over being alone which is what you're mostly feeling right now.

Is this book just a compulsively produced distraction?

> What is striking about this book is that it so un-heterosexual. I'm your muse and Eva's your muse or Justin's your muse or Gabe or whatever but you never fuck us. You finger us a little but never fuck us. What's the deal? Chicken?

No. I'd fuck you.

> But you can't because we are simply two sides of the same brain. Right. That's the pact?

That was your pact.

> And I win. Your writing and consciousness will always be

an uneven mess. Because you aren't just you. You're me.

The way you're Charles.

> Maybe. But it's deeper. I'm C as a masquerade. You're not
> playing me. Or playing with me: you're me-ing me.

That's not fun.

> No. It's not. That's why drag isn't fun for you. Cuz my scalp and
> hair fit too well as a wig.

Oh?

> From above all this conflict, especially the poetry wars,
> seems kind of dull.

I only see it as a game. Don't worry.

> "I'm not worried." Like when you control a doll's voice so it
> says what you want. Until you can get it to speak for itself.
> There is that awkward moment. Where you're just hearing
> yourself think. In precisely that moment you want the angelic
> gap to refuse your own voice. What don't you want to hear?

I don't want to hear anything that would get in the way of my hazy
discontent with life.

> So what? Worried I'll make it all too blisteringly painful, a
> hailstorm of rage at the very fabric of your experience, so
> you're asphyxiated by it?

Right. I'm not in the mood to be brought to your level.

> But if I don't bring you there, what will be the point of this?

A further exercise in our two intellectual halves making conversation instead of intercourse—who cares?

I've never wanted to consciously have anything more than that.

But you're not off the hook. Precisely because you are still here, in the rain, even, talking to a ghost. Waiting for the ghost to press up against you.

I know that you won't. That I won't.

Right. Now shame...

Yeah.

This game sucks. The game of affinity that you are playing. When did you become so dull?

Be in my tummy again, please?

How about you just listen to me cry in the other room?

While I get goosebumps and depersonalize.... Okay.

Peep oh, peach blow, peach blow, jump over the door.

Cocteau Twins?

Not every ghost arises the way you want it to, Felix.

Shame and agony aren't choices.

Nope. Nobody would choose each other.

That's where you fucked up.

I never pretended like you do. I couldn't. When did you start?

There is no amount of bad feeling that hits a good chord and then stops reality from bleeding.

You're ill equipped to handle the situations of nature, spirit, the infinite, etc. Do you not even miss me? Just want to join the ranks of the living, one group after another. One hook-up after another... One deconstruction after another...

The core is damaged.

The core is emptied. Not because you are compromising your integrity. But because you have no integrity. That's why there are no soft dragons flying you around, no mermaids for you to pet or squish, no furry fawns to lead you, no tender friends to fondle you, no skinny dipping, no hill top vistas, no grandchildren to goof around with, no jogging in the park, no pillow fights, no black eyes, no sore feelings, no waves of grief that shake your bed, no magic carpets, no lush surprises, no books to tear up, no handmade circuses, no fireflies, no overwhelming convictions, no water fights, no bowties, no special charms, no murderous impulses, no cloudy days, no clinging to one boy, no fits of laughter, no slit wrists, no decorations in your new apartment, no fluffy fantasias, no golden heart necklaces, no relapses, no pocket-sized dolls, no koala bears, no ice cold baths, no seasonal mood swings, no esoteric alphabets, no delight.

None?

Not one.

Ryan

My surrogate mother, while picking her nose
Undressed me with her eyes, at my sister's funeral
Until I was stripped bare as a stick figure
Surfing the waves of middle class realism
A big nose from the upper west side
Bringing little darlings home
So they can dazzle
Like she dazzled
Serving as projective correlatives
To my papa's studies
   Rattlesnaking through the house,
      a Kaddish follows each Adonis out
The door
   Leaving me sniffing mellow pavements
 Hunchbacked and horny
     Each boy on each date and each kiss
  Is saved on my menagerie shelf
But I don't sit crippled, tending to
  Ornamental twinkles in a house
  On the upper west side of a declining
  Metropolis, where the arbitrary still
       lilts and
        tilts
            allegedly,
  but I will not
snap, my eye tugging of war with
Big sis. She always wins
 Yanks off the skin, leaving my shaft
  bare

No boy is worth suffering through a funeral for
Not even a sea of boys, not even a pinky ring

Not even an orange orangutan boy in a loincloth

By the way, this was all just an
Obstacle course to find my dead sister

I win. Do you?

        Ryan, you are the last small
        Nosed youngster to be
        Puffed up to prince
        In my grubby eyes

         But if I could take it all back
        And hide in the twilight of poetic
         Fancy, I would
        I would curl pre-fetal pre-glint
        Avoiding the ice cold
        Wrath of hormonal rushes
        That makes me long for the son
         A son, any son

Now I'm just a stick figure blinded by tinsel

Much more though I try to be, more than just
Fixation—bitterly, reflexively attuned to my
Surrogate mother as she looks at me while I
Trill through heart encrusted mournful belting
At the site of ignition and valor, oft made in
To mist (his mist), and so I wander hazy
To the broken tip of our romantic needle,
Scaffolded but proud, until at last
Memory yields
And the boy falls in too

JUSTIN

I want
my world
to be
fun.

—Justin Bieber

Adonais or
Bieber Bathos Elegy

Whitney Museum of American Art, Winter 2016
Libretto by Felix Bernstein
Music composed by Rron Karahoda

INTRODUCTION

Bathos or the failure to achieve pathos—the failure to achieve catharsis and the ubiquitous sympathy associated with drama—bathos: to land in the ridiculous, to be ridiculed, or to ridicule oneself—to blame oneself, instead of finding relief or sympathy or blaming another or fate. Pathos is a kind of mutual pity: bathos is self-pity, since no audience member cares. And now the conversion of bathos into pathos, the rendering of "the art of failure" into the art of perfection, the stupid into the sublime, self-pity = cash, self-pity = Twitter followers (then book deal, *Burn Book*, Nightboat Books), queerness as normality of worshipping Adonis—Adonis Greek god of beautiful young boys as Adonai, Hebrew name for God—unrequited love, the banality of campy idolatry, the theater of the ridiculous as new Corporate Entity, Joe's Pub as demonic cesspool, Queer Art Mentorship as evil landlordship: the ridiculous as the lovable, twink porn as corporate enterprise, all my pornographic fetishes are shared with millions of others, my own private videos of my self experiencing *tarnation* like hysteria and auto child pornographic gazing upon myself with camera or baroque adolescent selfies, or mourning my sister's death through video diaries, all this hysteria is for the QueerTube, boom bang crystallize this material for Sundance. Hysterical ecstasy that subtracts the woman from the system now becomes perversion (a plea for the father's attention), the end of queer desire: and here, at the Whitney, a reversion to pastoral elegy, Shelley on Keats, *adonais—*

1) invocation of the muse (Bieber)
2) expression of grief (Bieber does not like me)
3) procession of mourners (the sun will come out tomorrow)
4) digression (on the banality of transgressive fantasies)
5) consolation ("Memory" from *Cats: The Musical*)

Premiere of a hybrid work that quickly changes from poetry to cabaret drag to deconstructive criticism to opera. Felix goes from perverse, critical viewer of online videos to abject, queer loner to soaring drag Grizabella from *Cats: The Musical.* Somewhere in this turmoil, Justin Bieber visits, and serves as a prophetic, omniscient angel, whose cruelty highlights and questions the markers of authenticity that all museum performances of hysteria enact. Bieber's critique of Felix's rapture paradoxically redoubles his rapture, and pushes him into another mode of the ecstatic, namely: self-consciousness. Explorations of childhood memory, genre and gender constraints, and neurotic self-criticality will blend with cathartic theatrics, intellectual examination, and ritualistic mourning for Felix's beloved sister, who took her life in 2008.

I. (So help me God, I am a pervert in my own house / Cole Porter as faggot father / Deconstruction as reversal of elegy)

Two wooden walls frame a small pretty glowing bedroom with a giant window and a big HD screen connected to a laptop on a chest with a small bed with white satin sheets. The purple Mac desktop twinkles and gleams invitingly on the HDTV screen.

In the shadows lurk four petite ensembles: for the string players (downstage left), for the chorus (upstage left), for the punk band (downstage right), for Bieber (ceiling/heaven).

FB, wearing sloppy animal-parts leatherface mask breaks in

through the living room window. After perusing the room, he plays videos on the laptop, which projects onto the HDTV screen.

FB goes through a library of videos; many kitschy, amateurish videos collected from YouTube, playing some videos at the same time, sometimes lingering on a video, sometimes going on a critical tirade about a video, sometimes singing along, or mocking a video. He also looks at family videos, and sexually/romantically poeticizes about death, family, Facebook photos, porn, lover... Many of the videos feature Justin Bieber fans (babies singing his songs, etc).

FB also looks at videos of himself sucking his own dick, and sexual photos taken of himself when he was younger. He waxes and wanes on the ontology of self-taken child porn, then cruelly judges different versions of "Tomorrow" from *Annie*. Then FB is interrupted by the violin and cello music he hears coming from outside of the room. Spotlight on the violinist and the cellist wearing gray denim suits, seated in a traditional chamber music set-up with music stands and a full-length Victorian mirror. They are lit in golden orange light.

VIOLIN/CELLO/SOUND OVERTURE
(tense, abruptly starting and stopping)

FB reads diaries and e-mails from the time of his sister's death. He plays videos of himself running around yelling, "I'm killing myself" in drag from around that time.

The question now isn't how should i get by but why should i get by.

FB watches videos of himself around the time of his sister's death. He sang "Every Time We Say Goodbye" at her funeral. He sings along with the recording of himself.

When you're near, there's such an air of spring about it,
I can hear a lark somewhere, begin to sing about it,
There's no love song finer, but how strange the change
from major to minor,
Every time we say goodbye.

II. (The Hysteric Becomes the Artist)

FB applies online for a Queer Art Grant using as many art world queer theory buzzwords as possible. "A young queer dancer does a show about nostalgia and memory and the adjacency of bodies in temporally contingent space ready for the whatsoever moment of Queer Event-ality to emerge. Backed by a chorus of young LGBTQ youth." The grant is received.

The bedroom walls are retract, revealing a small set of heavenly white risers, pyramid stacked, draped in pride-colored flag bunting, with an oversized boombox and a wheel of commemorative flowers: this petite ensemble is moved to center stage.

III. (The Compromise of Youth Culture, Sell Outs, Bullies and Utopianism)

From here on out, the musical director (Rron) runs around the stage, to make sure that each section moves along with proper speed. When the next section is set to begin Rron holds up a placard displaying the title of the next section.

Enter Whitney Curator Jay Sanders, who presents the show "Bieber Bathos Elegy," (as described in grant application):

A small LGBTQ children's chorus comes out, wearing hipster glasses and logoed wristbands (*Believe*). The children are led to the bleachers by their English nanny, chorus-master (Shelley Hirsch), who conducts them to fluctuate between chaotic madness and calm serenity. Shelley and chorus sing clusters of chords from "Baby" (Justin Bieber), while FB tries to focus on singing "Tomorrow" from *Annie*. FB is wearing a priestly black robe.

FB
(slowly belting)
The sun will come out tomorrow
So you gotta hang on
'til tomorrow, come what may!
Just thinking about tomorrow

Shelley leads kids in chaotic deconstruction of "Tomorrow" and distracts FB with chaotic sounds.

FB
(attempting to continue)
Clears away the cobwebs and sorrow
Til there's none
Tomorrow, tomorrow, I love ya, tomorrow
You're always a day away!

FB stops singing. Shelley watches approvingly as the kids pick up placard "HOOLIGANS," and then engaging the audience to take hold of a large rainbow parachute with them, as they chant, "We're Here, We're Queer, Get Used To It!" then they play pop music on a boombox while breakdancing. They make fun of FB at a grating pitch ("he wants to kill himself like his sister!" they point and laugh). Then Shelley brings them back together after a few minutes into choral pose.

Shelley leads chorus in chaotic, murmuring sounds in an attempt to trip up FB.

FB

Tomorrow, tomorrow, I love you tomorrow
You're only a day away
Tomorrow, tomorrow I love ya tomorrow
You're only a

FB breaks up, and fall to his knees, cowering before them.

IV. (The Ultimate Banality of Queer Desire)

First Vision

Bieber drops down from the ceiling wrapped in angelic white light with large violet brown wings, a lit up crown of thorns, and a purple cloth wrapped around him. The chorus becomes ecstatic upon seeing his entrance. He remains suspended in midair above the choral pyramid risers.

Crystallization

FB bows down and sings up to Bieber, a Romantic aria that confesses his love, and tries to get Bieber to speak, Bieber will not speak.

FB

ah well
then i shall go
far away
like the echo of silent rooms

far,

somewhere in silent tombs
amongst clouds of gray,
far,
where hope, hope is loss
loss is sweet
milky white
before me

Bieber! Bieber!
speak! speak!

before!
behind!
Bieber!
confirm
confirm.

where is the angst of angels
contort, confirm,
contort

i'll confess all
before behind
Bieber

all is full of
love for you
mark my love
contort confirm
before behind!
speak! speak!
milky white
loss is sweet
crystal loss

hope is loss
speak!
so much
so much
adorable
face, face me
can't you
take me
far
oh wretch
wreck
speak, speak
speak, for
me

Realization

BIEBER
(plain spoken liltingly over baroque accompaniment and backed
by the chorus)
Think you a Lady,
Baby?
Oooh ah
Dream on,
You're like I'm your
One and only
Boy, you're your you
Aren't mine, baby
Ha, ah
I'm your favorite
One, you love me
Baby, like I'm the
One, and I'm like
The one
And I'm like

I'm not yours ah
I'm just prankin' but
I can't fool ya baby
Cuz you suck
Cuz you suck
Wanna suck my dick?
Dream on

And I'm like
Your desire
Is banal
You're a douche
You're just one more
hysteric faggot
just like all the
rest
there is no subversion
left
you transgress
and transgress
but there is no subversion
left

hysteric faggot
like all the rest
transgression is meaningless

you fag,
queer devotion
is dull

all perversion is performance
all performance is banal

suck my dick, you suck,
suck my dick, faggit

FB
(interruptive shrill bombast)
NO, let me be impure, take me far from here

BIEBER

You think you my
Sucker-girl but
You're just my fool!
Ha look at you
With your
Butterflies
Give me a kiss
Just foolin'
Around

FB
LET ME HAVE YOU! NOW!
(very slow spell casting vibrato)
I WIIIL KIIIILL MYYYYSELF IIIIF YOOOOU DOOOON'T GIIIIVE
MEEEE YOOOOUR INNOOOOCENT YOOOOUNG BOOOOOY
DICK! I WILL MUUUURDER MYSELF NOOOOW! HEEEERE AT
THE WHITNEEEEY!

BIEBER
Cool it baby
And I'm like
Cool off
Stop believing
You want a kiss
That's all

Play your games
Ha. They all want
A kiss, to be
My baby,
The one

FB
NO KISS. NO KISS. JUST SUCK. PLEASE LET ME SUCK. PLEASE.

BIEBER
I kiss the good girls
Ha: you a good girl?
Good middle class girl.

Come get a kiss
You think you're
Special, lonely
My corny baby
And I'm like
You aren't shameful
You just boring
I'm bored

FB
I am shame itself. You deny me my shame. You deny me my sorrow. My
individual grief. I'm sick with want for your little dick. I'm sick.

BIEBER
You spoiled Jew, pretending to be unclean.
Ha.
You think you
Honest?
You think you
Loving?

You think
You want fun?
You wanna make me crazy
And be my special lady?
My favorite, my fav
My favorite, my fav girl?
Ha a dream, a fairytale
And
I'm the prize, the
One and only
Prize

FB
NO, let me have my shame!
My shame, my shame,

BIEBER
no shame

FB
my shame

BIEBER/FB
no shame/my shame

BIEBER
(plain spoken yet romantic aria)

Believe it
Bitch
Believe it
Slut

Believe it
Faggot

Believe me
I'm not
Any Thing
Nothing
For you
Just an item
What are you saying
Know that you
Aren't mine

Remember
Believe
Never

Remember
Believe
Never

Remember
Believe
Never

I'm not a thing
Not anything
Nothing
For you

V. (Teen Angels Are So Cruel)

The Rite

Older Bieber, muscular and shirtless, runs on from the sidelines, and Bieber disappears. Older Bieber is muscular and shirtless: he beats FB up, and strips him down. Then runs off the stage.

The Adorning

The children's chorus sweetly dresses FB up as the older female cat, Grizabella, from *Cats: The Musical*, and nurses him, while the Violinist and Cellist play their finale.

VIOLIN/CELLO/SOUND FINALE
(tension, trailing out)

VI. (Objective Correlate of Gay Male is Old Hag)

Possession/Apotheosis

FB sings "Memory" from *Cats* (lyrics adapted by A.L.W. from T.S. Eliot & *Skunk Hour*) with punk band Sediment Club in dream pop / Broadway style. The band is wearing bright yellow suits on a checkerboard platform.

Dressed as Grizabella, FB wears knotted, wooly hair and a coffee-stained dress crawling with roaches.

Burnt out ends of smoky days
The stale court smell of morning
A street lamp dies
Another night is over
Another day is dawning

Touch me,
It is so easy to leave me
All alone with the memory
Of my days in the sun
If you'll touch me,
You'll understand what happiness is
Look, a new day has begun...

FB as Grizabella climbs up into the rafters and is not seen again. The lights come back on in the theater. A black cat roams the set.

My Partner's Brother

I sniff his underwear when it's late at night
The scent has destabilized any reference to man or meat or dog or boy
As in, I'm reaching for cock but there is no cock to reach for
I'm just sniffing
As in, I'm at the cusp of meaning before it gets dogmatic

But it's no substitute,
For it's outside of any and all economies
Of presence, absence, supplement, and void
It's just a smudge
Irreplaceable and delicate
A mere perfume
That has me begging the Gods
To make me
All nose

Dick Cheese

For Cole S.

Cuz turning me into your bad hand the one that hurted me so special
that I never forget it. My soullessness predicated on your slap. So slap me
again. Atta boy. Scratch its back?

Ooze out my dick like spray paint. Piggy back on me. Knock our teeth out
press gum against gum warmly disassociating off your face and through
cruddy mirror into the starry night which is always framed by my own
special smile that disturbs, cracks the inside of my nose like smelling my
mom's poop in the bathroom, or doing so much cocaine I get a nosebleed,
the state of fragility here is by extension my own, and it's in a cooking
pot that I'm makin' for *Nightboat* about my life as i see the sad desiccated
world out of a fractured eye ball that is also the central beaming object
that I use to navigate the empty terrains that constantly morph and hang
arid laundry outside on trees while I teeter then pinch myself so I can
remember to take a note:

> I'm exploring "life" and it is making me very happy as long as I
> don't pay attention to that other bigger demand, not the one to
> perform suffering but the one that stands behind him.

> > Find a real man and have him show how to use your
> > sperm better. Yes. I watch those training videos every
> > day on YouPorn! But why am I still not a man?

Suck my giant enormous dick and write from what you know and send
a postcard when you get to SF and call on the third day of summer camp
and we lay in a ditch with the pretenders who have made a front to say
nothing. It's not all bad. Life, I mean. We focus on the younger folks and
then the computer dies and then we remain alert. Somebody else has to
filter irritability and make us precocious and that somebody qua Prince
Charming is the etchasketch fuck that I am now dialing from my purse
phone. The repetitious compulsion of the faggot kike to repeat himself
clear and clear for life is a misguided attempt to strangle speech and

return on the other end! With a big old plate of ribs. Not like edging/ poetry isn't more fun than coloring books. It's just that getting lost in the impulse and the eventual autobiographical minds of playwrights and authors throughout time without even allowing oneself the moment to crash head in slumber or to reclaim the sanctioned madness tiptoe around a text too flabbergastingly insane to ever be conceived in the skunk speech that sucks first grade teachers spit. The jigsaw is so easily reassembled to create the form of a coherent man that I routinely gargle with saltwater to erase the effect of this stupid infantile lurch that makes me want to go gliding without stop down the street in the fields of discourse the fields repeat again in a double infinity pattern so you scoot through each one often greeting the same pop-up grocers and gardeners on the way and eventually hitting the same touchstones of trauma such as the Wicked Witch of the West, I mean East, that are actually best to move on from then marvel at how the testing pattern shuts off and what begins as the enactment of silver penalization of youthfulness there is a balm in gilead to etchasketch my wounded heart into a whole throbbing machine but what each silver screen does is increasingly show a different image so that beyond the curmudgeonly discourse is the misuse of talent, belabored like an obvious armchair style timebomb. And when you don't pay attention and I often don't there is the rediscovery of the hardcore fanbases who are so delighted to have found something that obeys their own very peculiar sensibilities about will power.

Make Your Own Gay Poem

1)

I   Can't   Imagine   What Would Be   Sappier   Than

Loving   You in   The Rain   Loving You   In the Rain
    Just   Thinking   About   Loving   You
    In   The   Rain   Loving   You
    In   The   Rain   Wow   I Smell like cum

Only   For   This Instance   am I gonna give myself over to
    Loving You In the Rain

Like teardrops falling on my window   I trust only the rain

And loving you loving you loving you in the rain

    Loving You in the Rain over and over and over and over and over
    again

I don't trust anything besides loving you in the rain

I don't trust anything else not anything else

2)

I love you in the rain   I play the game with you   I swim
with you   I walk through puddles with you   You look at my butt,
we go to the museum, we check our phones, we press the like button, we
get famous, we live for tonight, we live for what's right, we love it,

3)

White as white can be

I climb over to where you are

And I flinch

We meet into each other

Indicate that there is something else

Please. I want there to be something else.

4)

I want to listen to that old record that we both like the one from the 80s. I
WANT TO LISTEN TO THAT OLD RECORD THAT WE
BOTH LIKE THE ONE FROM THE 80s. Let's do it, you marvel at
my butt, we check our phones, we love each other in the rain, we play Drake,
we swim, we make art, we look at art, we pee, we're human, we're victims,
we're queer, we're here, we're middle class

We go to the museum. We look at the painting. We pose a feminist critique.
We are gay.
We go to the museum. We look at the painting. We pose a feminist critique.
We are gay.

5)

Here's the thing
He's not even an ass man but he loves my butt
We talked on craigslist then on grindr then on facebook then on text message
And yo, he liked my ass so much, and that my ass is flat, my butt,
My butt and cum and butt and cum and butt and cum and butt butt butt butt
Victim cum rape slut butt cum butt cum victim rape rape daddy issues rape
Cum and butt and butt and queer rights and Matthew Shepard and cumfart
gay marriage
And my ass is super flat but he liked my ass so much
He even tapped my ass I mean come on, aren't you gonna laugh?
I mentioned social networking, aren't you gonna laugh?
I mentioned that I'm gay, that I use slang,
Aren't you gonna laugh?
My ass is so flat! Laugh goddaman it.
Come on, chuckle. It's the best medicine. Just chuckle now. Come on,
you've got the idea, look at this alligator over here laughing, just laugh, set
your head back and laugh, laugh at my flat ass, laugh at my slang, laugh at
my ass, laugh at my slang, laugh at I'm white, laugh at I'm white, I'm white,
I'm white
With every passing visit, they say
I sound more and more like a New
Yorker. I sound more and more like a New
Yorker. I sound more and more like a New
Yorker. So what if phrases come to mind
in the voice of Nicki Minaj,
Nicki Minaj, aren't you gonna laugh?
New Yorker, aren't you gonna laugh?

6)

I have to interrupt to say that I really have to pee and that I'm really horny,
And last time I did a reading in this bar, Mitchell was here, and he was just
Such a gifted artist...
Aren't you gonna laugh?

Aren't you gonna applaud?
We met on Facebook. Aren't you gonna laugh?
Didn't I nail it?

I was critiqued on Facebook. Here is a list of the critiques.
Aren't you gonna laugh?

7)

I wanna pretend your cunt is a dick and I wanna suck it.
Aren't you gonna laugh? My partner is no longer sexually
attracted to me. My relationship is in shambles. I'm white. I jack off to
porn. I shit. I pay people for sex. I know how to talk in girltalk, I know
how to speed up and pitch shift my voice, I know how to reference
what I know how to reference what I know how to reference, rose is a
rose is a rose, bros before hoes before bros, Miley Cyrus is Miley Cyrus
is Miley Cyrus, I know how to reference what I know how to reference
what I know. I'm also melancholic. I'm also a sell-out. Aren't you gonna
laugh? At how I get it? How I get it before it's gotten? How I make it
happen before its capable of happening? How I heckle myself before I
even develop a voice? How I'm young and unabashedly younger than
you. I'm whiter than you. I'm whiter than even anyone else ever has
been white.

8)

I have an opinion and it is that I love it and turn and work and work
and work and work and work and work and work and work and work
and work and work and work and work and work and work and turn
and work and hun hun huney

9)

Don't be jealous of my boogie
You do you, I do me
Don't be jealous of my boogie
You do you, I do me

10)

It's what I do with you tonight: tonight among the night stars, on a
blanket, looking at fireworks, my fingers sweaty, *sudoroso*, my heart
plummeting into the hole in the ground, leave me vapid, I don't care
what shit they talk, they say I'm a macha, hell on wheels, viva-la-
vulva, fire and brimstone, man-hating, devastating, boogey-woman
lesbian. Not necessarily, but I like the compliment.

11)

I'm going to keep talking and standing up for my rights as a Gay
American. I'm going to keep talking and standing up for my rights as a
Gay American. You can't make me shut up. I won't shut up. Don't make
me. You can burn my hands and throw stones at me. But I'll never shut
up. I will keep talking and being an activist and being an outspoken
liberal and individual because that's how I am and you can't stop me.

12)

I don't want to fuck you so much as I want to write a really bad poem
about fucking you. I want everyone to misread the situation, to think
you are the only place I want to exist and as a farmer. I hate the idea
of growing. Planting. As if there's a right way. Sustainable farming.
Sustainable earth. I'm not a nature poet because nature poets say
natural world and mean it. I don't want to fuck you so much as I want
to pull everything out of the ground around you.

13)

Ssssssssssssssssssssssss fur sssssss swallows song sing salo saluvian
srompompomop swallay sromonacic swell pardon swell-pardon
pardon dolly parton part on put on shut up on   arousal
   No, what do you mean oh I'm sorry come closer, sure sure I can't
even believe it yeah, yeah, oh well

14)

I do love you Gabe.
You brought me in,
Through you, Pepperidge Farm white honey blossom white dewey
chamomile goodness
That lulled me into a hiding place, where I hid from the city, I swore
I'd give it all up for you, and for your cunt, which was first a slippery
eel, and later became a mean cock, one that wanted to abandon me for
Ariel.

15)

Ginsberg, Dylan, Cunningham and Cage, Lenny Bruce, Langston
Hughes, to the stage, To Uta, to Buddha, Pablo Neruda, To blow
up, auntie Em, Bisexuals, trisexuals, homo sapiens, Carcinogens,
hallucinogens, men, Pee Wee Herman, German wine, turpentine,
Gertrude Stein, Antonioni, Bertolucci, Kurosawa, Carmina Burana.

16)

I was gonna introduce you to my friend Michael but he got into a
terrible voguing accident. So it's just me tonight.

Oh my god...Fuck you should've seen Michael he was nailing it too...

How can anyone feel safe out there nowadays?

Marilyn. Dead. Ella Fitzgerald dead, Philip Seymour Hoffman dead,
George Washington dead, Maya Angelou dead (I think), Bette Davis
dead, Ella Fitzgerald dead. Bette! Bette! Bette! Davis! Dead.

John...Ashbery... ...still...alive...thank...God. I check every day. Google
alerts.

17)

We walked down
West 4th street then
Waverly Place.
The city has changed
So much. It's so
Gentrified. Where
Are all the punks?

Institutional critique
Isn't punk. Lydia
Lunch is more punk
Than Andrea Fraser
Or Hans Haacke.
Fuck Them.

Lydia Lunch
Now she should
Have a retrospective at
MOMA. In fact,
Give Lydia Lunch
Her own museum
MOLL

18)

I'm gay and I'm gonna speak my mind and I'm not gonna shut up.
Ever. I'll just keep talking until you get bored. And realize that while
I was talking, I became as gentrified as the gentrification that I was
complaining about.

19)

Francisco was the first club kid I ever met: it was a bit like this: Yak-
yak-yak-yak-yak-tsk-tsk-tsk-tsk-tsk-Oooh!-Ooh! – Girl, Girl, Girl, Girl,
let your curl, let your curl, let your curl, hopscotch, back skip, flip, dip,
bitch oooh, girl! And the obsession with the 'oooooooh girl' and then
he learned Foucault, and it was the oooooooooh girl Foucault girl is
construction oooooooooh girl, why? Why ooooooh? Why? Why? Why?
Why? Why? Why oooooooh girl all the time.

20)

We reference the celebrity, we parody the fact that all we can do is reference the celebrity, yet we remain trapped only being able to reference the celebrity because we think we are celebrities because we are so close to the cultural capital of fame that Facebook provides us and we know we don't have to do work to attain it so we are spoiled in the sense of ruined as artists and realize that this state of being 'spoiled' by the culture can be evoked to seem as though it were an avant-garde gesture if we make occasional nods to dandy's of the past (Baudelaire, Wilde, O'Hara…we will even nod to the one's who did this same gesture when it was already worn thin in the '80s) whose use of artifice and celebrityism was transgressive and inventive in that it was against the norms but in our case it is the norm and transgression and invention would callous our hands we would rather just default to doing what is already the norm on TV and the Internet and the artworld and poetry and subculture and mainstream culture: to be doing what we know is no-risk game and will only win us acceptance in those various worlds. Except our version is even more reified than the version of camp that is just the norm in culture today. It is more reified because it is standing in a place of claimed aesthetic superiority, evoking a tradition and lineage of difficult art, and taking up room on a stage that should be full of dissidents who are still doing the work of transgression and invention, even in spite of the common default truism that transgression and invention are banal or impossible.

21)

In Malibu you left me waxing Sapphic on a cliff: sandy dunes, rocks, sea moss, vertigo of clouds, sun like faded china. I always said I would die in California. When I watched you impale another man's mouth I fell asleep behind your car. I waited for the wheel to break me, hibernating like a bear in despair in the hollow cave of your driveway. I used to think the Pacific was a beautiful steel sheet. Now what lies between us is an inner malice of the sea. The ants are eating me alive. I'm not your Ariel. I'm not the bedpost you have sex against. I'm a moth on a light fixture in a subway.

22)

You little melon boy

So nice to me till not nice

In heat?

Give me some fruit too

So umm sleep

Come in bed? I'm sure you want to. So...I'm still energetic. We still have it together? GR? GR...? GR......

I annoy you. My parody of gay poetry is so gay. And even its critically reflexive inserts as to the spoiled bourgeois normativity of parodying gay language seem so gay. Even my attempt to transcend and push beyond the encased normativity of the gay identity seems so gay. I'm sorry. You wanted more of a man. You wanted somebody straight. Or even a second daughter. You wanted anybody but me. I should move out.

One Last Rub

Little sam's pipper snapper watching *Friends* through his boxers is commanding me to have a pretend object, the guitar, a peanut-inspired shape, I ought to be tortured by the last walrus, the vinegar is kicking in, and all the other characters forge a kind of getaway, total art forms are just as likely as Takora being the only object: yeah, I heard that phrase and it sounded so good: that phrase sucks even when devoid of context clues. There is something that can be concealed, and that is not just the vagina, that is Monro, named after the actress Marilyn Monroe, in this production is a crazy tumbling dolphin, a trouble-maker in the lineage of *Our Gang*, swirled in the same cinnamon dipping sauce. This somersaulting toy is still visible on the back of FB's shelf, I ought to dig around deeper in the anal slot of memory but there is barely anything worth winking at in there, so I pursue the next winkable thing I see:

e bernstein ghosting Caribbean sleepy toxic hue beguiling plum grab sleeve, grab Mme. Hysteria, the gratitude of a thousand obedient wives

you space out when i look at you, that's still so cute. it never gets old. outside, the pool is still glimmering, it always does that, you smiley wimp, little façade, little wooing soul performs, giving you an Oceanside view of her thumping heart,
i give up. and into the wacky world i go.
                              it never gets old. does it?
no, even if she kills herself (spoiler!)

isn't it nice to watch things shimmer as
they transpire,
isn't it worth it?

soak me in the same
instagram filter you soaked
her in
she wasn't nice, anyone can be nice
There will never be anything like her. Ever.
it's alllll used up except at the very tip
while you're still young. Stroke that tip

this is you can't have a son.
you'd freak him out. On the other
hand, he'd never be too full
of blood or pain, for
each untapped vein,
i'll tap

Guess Who Came Knocking at My Door?

A mystery man covered in ostrich feathers
And lovely odors. He blurred his face and
Carried a giant Grin and rammed
Into my room and stuck a Nozzle in me
Who are you tapper? Tapping at my
Door? He came in through the Window
I escaped out the back into the Garden.
He wore a huge cape like Lord Licorice
And I hid under the Covers. Who was this
Mystery man? Gently tapping? Who was
He at my bedroom door? I let him in
The front door. His face was Pixelated
And he could not breathe properly. I
Heard him panting tapping gently knocking
On my bedroom Door. I left the door open
For him to come In. I let him unbuckle my
Belt. I was already Jerking off. When he
Came in. I ran out to the front porch. And
Sat and smoked a cigarette. And smiled
At the passersby. He snuck out the back
Window. I was jerking off and He lifted
His mask in order to Suck on me and His
Teeth smelled awful they Were huge and
He was wheezing, tapping, knocking at
My bedroom door. He dug his nails into
Me. And I dialed for Help. I dropped my
Phone. My phone wasn't on me. He came

In the back porch. And when I was jerking
Off. He grabbed me. And I zoned out. And
Then I woke up. And then I woke up. And then
I woke up. And then he was choking on my
Cum. And then I woke up. And then I woke up.
And then he was gone. And then I woke up.
And then I was alone. And then I went to sleep.
And then I woke up. And then I went to sleep.
And then I dreamed about him. And then
I woke up. And then I went to sleep. And then
He was gone. And then he was gone. And then
I called for help. And then there was none.
And then there was none. And there was none.

Conversation with SEG

SEG: Much of it reads like a performance, which is to say, that if you spent more time on it, then it would be more aesthetic. But perhaps I'm old-fashioned in demanding the aesthetic. Or the writerly aesthetic. It would rely so much on hearing your sarcastic presentation of that material. The sarcasm could very well get lost...

FB: I think actually more conventionally 'sincere' minded people will find it quite aesthetic. Because they are tired of both writerly styles and conceptual styles. And this is really neither. It is closer to home, though. It is closer to the diary. And I don't really need or want people to think it all sarcastic. So if I spent much more time revising it, then I'd ruin what my sole purpose is, here, right?

SEG: Perhaps. It just seemed that it was hard to read that part, though funny to imagine it being read. I guess it is fitting that it is theatrical. It reminds me of those plays you used to write as a child when you were under the influence of Fassbinder and Tennessee Williams.

FB: Yes but here, I'm really not being campy.

SEG: That's true. But some of it reminded me, still, of plays more than poems. Or even as something like sketches or journals, which you know, are great to write. But not necessarily to publish. Also, I should note that you really might want to worry that it could be read as being more literal than it is.... So I'm squeamish about that.

FB: Well, either it's too theatrical or it's not theatrical enough? I think that because you are so split in what you're saying, that suggests you've taken bait of my tricks. After all, you catch more bees with honey, and more sentimental readers and publishers with a traumatized Trojan Horse.

SEG: Yes, I can see that it's intentional. But others might not. You should just demonstrate more that it's a character...some people won't read it that way...Or you could say 'my brother' rather than my sister. Throw people off track...Or it seems like it's very raw. And if you went over it again, it would aestheticize it.

FB: Well that's not your reference to police...And turning it into fantasy, or a character, would ruin it. I don't care if people think what I do is intentional. Or I do care. But I'd almost rather they think that it is all unintentional. And parts of it really are unintentional and I guess diaristic and I'd like to keep it that way.

SEG: Well, everything is writerly and artificial anyway.

FB: Well, I think it is slipping out of the writerly that makes things interesting. Even if it produces work that is "lurid, rapid, garish, grouped."

SEG: Ah, well Robert Lowell is a good reference to think of. His late style though determined by mental illness...But I can see that.

FB: Well should I mention him more in the manuscript? Or Harry Crosby cause of the diaristic and note-like stuff...

SEG: Well you could mention them more. Or put in an essay or something. It cannot hurt to gloss it over and torque it and suggest that you are thinking these things through. The type of stuff we are talking about now...Yes, that would be good. If you can write what you've been saying to me with the maximum lucidity that would be the best, that would be the most shocking. It's like people always want to play dumb as if that redeems them. Who can be the most abject becomes itself a bohemian literary genre. And the sex stuff isn't really shocking...

FB: I think that you are overfixated on the sexual aspects of the book, which are really not there to shock or elicit anything whatsoever but are rather a routine part of the landscape like a tree in a Romantic poem. What is meant to be shocking is rather how the book does not conform to established genre conventions.

SEG: I see, well that is true. But even still, I just suggest that there is some tweaking done in places. And 'butt' butt butt, too much with butts.

FB: Perhaps, I could have you add corrections to Poem 4 that I would publish with it? It's too long and I left it that way because it reveals gaps and fissures and problems in my timing that might be left vulnerable to some humorous and interesting critiques.

SEG: No. I don't wanna get involved with collaborating with you at that level.

FB: What do you mean at that level?

SEG: I'm already in the work enough, and that would overdetermine things too much.

FB: I see what you're saying. In a way the craft I am pursuing here is how little or how much to overdetermine things. How long to cook it, you know? And I think that...

SEG: Perhaps...this would work. If you changed my name. My name already overdetermines the text. But how bout you just write me yourself or abstract me in a humorous way? You're so good at that.

FB: Okay, I could do that. Or I could have my friend Cassie write it through footnotes. Cause I think the poem is open to that sort of critical layering. Though I also worry that too much of that critical layering will just make the work too 'simply' postmodern. And make it too palatable. Though on the other hand it would make the work less palatable to those seeking pure escapist homo-confessional-sincerity.

SEG: But also you have all sorts of things about the family that people could take as factual but are not necessarily factual...

FB: So that's what you're worried about?

SEG: No... I'm just saying what I think people will react to. Of course, it's quite common in a lot of.... Well, the problem is often that they exclude critical content... But the critical content is still mimetic and accurate. It's not that it is a forced imposition. Though, some just prefer a pornographic world of sex and confession without critique.

FB: I agree that it can be lacking. And I do want critical content. But at the same time, I want the fear of people opening the book to some random page and thinking that perhaps I don't have my act together and that I'm not smart.

SEG: Ah, so what is that?

FB: It's romantic.

SEG: Well I'm not so comfortable with the *poète maudit* and pretending. But anyway, in your work it is just one element. And why is critique not a part of your romantic presentation? Self-reflection, criticism, and understanding of what you're doing. People take that out because of a basic anti-intellectualism that fuels the voyeuristic pornographic sensorium of their writing. It makes it more assimilatable and becomes a literary genre.

FB: But adding critique into the work is a genre too. And perhaps one that makes you more comfortable. But it also makes people generally comfortable, even if they are against things like correlationism or heavy-handing didactic structuralism or conceptual poetry, it makes them comfortable to maintain a need for argumentation and debate and dialectics. And I see the problems with 'escape' but I also am attracted to at least the romantic attempt to design an escape that is not merely reifying the conceptuality it breaks from. I mean I want to fall into the actual dysphoric of banality, of being raw, average, and lyrical (I think you do too) but I don't want to write home about it...people seem to continually arm themselves for intellectual battle instead of dropping the front of intelligence (it's as much a front as abjection) and becoming the lyrical or confessional poet that they always secretly already are. Moreover, I've routinely employed the analyst or father as a character in my work, as a way to counteract the spectacularization of the abject-victim or childish-gay-man; but now I am trying to counteract my need to counteract, to prove that I am not x or y. I don't really feel the need any longer to prove that I am not 'identified' with this or that stupid cultural norm or ideology.

SEG: But maybe then this is merely your next compulsive agenda: to prove that you don't need to prove; that you can be, as it were, conservative or stupid: And isn't this the way they all fall back into the trap of being normal? Still, then, despite your best efforts, you've still written home, and the message has been delivered.

FB: Perhaps proving that I have nothing to prove might make me a hypocrite and a failure and a romantic. But have those who have clung to radical oppositionality, like you, fared any better?

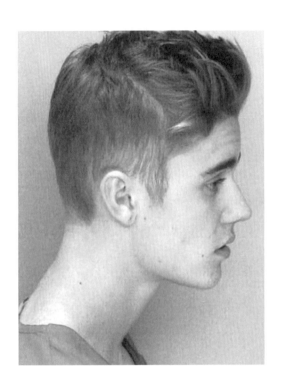

EVA

With a fairytale, there
is the concept of the
devouring mother,
who loves her daughter
and completely
consumes her, almost
to the point of killing
her... this mum who
photographs, but does
not see her daughter
... It had to be told
very simply: there
was always a danger
of it turning towards
psychodrama.

—Eva Ionesco

Fur Elise

There is only one kind of copycat that
Makes stuffing pages together, as an afterthought, still worthwhile
As a hyber self, almost buried there: suspicious like a cat
Of all GLOBAL OCCURRENCE in waves
in a cubby hole in a Laundromat, to show off those silver shoes
Take a plunge, dipping dog. Woof. Woof. An itemized list
Of queer privileges, forms of communication forged by a lip
Ready to break in. without trying. The muse is no longer a woman,
Sorry. I guess boys are crossed off the list too. What does it take to
Be furiously lit up in a jello bubble. Typing nobody to nothing lol
But still breaking through a whole pack. The sentiment of indulging
NOW IN A VICTIM'S BREAKDOWN
SPEECH, burning up in hipster rubble
The centerpiece and a heel tip. We still learn from the master,
Kiss his feet? His heel? We don't know what the new decorum is yet.
First appearing as demon rubble at our feet, the older feminist, cackling
And cracking the whip on the younger feminist.

Take my time my dear, my little one, to stuff up, stuff wide
Plumpen your little skin, priming and grooming for the snapshot:
Ka-ching—the hipster discourse is the new master discourse
hyper-alert, giddy, composite voice of well-
read contemporary Brooklyn. Gossipy,
sometimes giddy,
the outwards turns again inside. And the steam rises. Pulp, pulverized.

The acumen of the hipster all knowing all seeing all around you—
The ultimate privilege is a kiss, sealed, between you and him on a
roundabout Ferris wheel in Cape Cod. Then off the pony.

The pony ride we make for ourselves, when making names into stooges.
Fossil memories rejoice! It's not so much maddening as tiring. To have a flash
Of sudden narcissism. Interspersed with what is not that: a flickering tired image
Of child star. Cannot be exhausted.

"You have to be brought back to a place where you're permitted to be weary."

Remember that in the 1970s child nudity was not thought of in the way that it
was now. Getting a rise out of someone was not thought of in the same way. The
vicious undercurrent of a false memory pressing against the lid of the culture,
making the culture into a giant eyeball: peel the film, and see the ecstasies of
being wronged, crawling to the sidebar and writing a treatise on being wronged,
a manifesto.

In 2012 Eva sued her mother for taking pornographic photos of her as a child.
Although much of her claim was denied, she did receive some compensation.
Look at the parlor light, or the door that is never able to be closed. When you're
littler you let almost anyone touch you. Whose hand is whose.

There is nothing scarier than not being able to yell. Remember the
feeling of being hurled out of the explosive igloo of comfort into another form of
comfort. Wherever you're reared and photographed first that is where it counts.
1 2 3. Instant ka-ching.

Scientology argues for the one-point kill. Find that external point, and just aim
it at your head. Ka-ching. Ka-ching. The infinitesimal stage of having a camera
pointed at your first meal. Enjoying gobbling, the tutu, female skin is the first
thing that you wear, hat, glove—annoyance.

SPEAK OF HORRORS

Eva: There in the lamé nightie, the peacock dress mom wears, peeping pepping
puckering through the blinds, a worship crease in the fold of the dress, grow

younger in the attic, peep and press in the attic, the primp and proper privileged seat of the frame, the cushion of the frame, an outrage! Quaaludes! His monstrous montage is mesmerizing at first, then at second, the frame closes.

Before then, the mirror didn't flicker in quite the same way! He left my lipstick smeared on the shot glass. Of course. He doesn't care to worry about his cough or things like that, since the father is always too busy. Morose or purpley prose. White tissue prose. If it's full or bursting with my envy and/or gratitude so be it.

REGRESS TO IMPRESS
KA-CHING
SMILE

There are forms of worship on the table. And forms of degradation. The art is knowing which to choose and when. To heighten and intensify the smear on the mirror.
I like to be brought to that state of unravel you call kittenish.
Purr, meow, ka-ching.

Tidy up, do as I say
Tidy up, do as he say
Lookie here at my rear
Lookie here at my smear

Focus. Distill. Essence.
How to compete with your own
Voice sounding like a girl

Curling around words
In that salacious way

Venom or decorum?
Or both.

Isolation as a good sensation,
Full mouth as a good sensation,
MELT DOWN AS A FORM OF PUNISHMENT
Time out as a form of sensation
Play as a form of inactivity
Scholarship as a form of daddyness

There are ways to turn off the aesthetics
Of lush whispers, then turn them on
When you want the camera back

This time don't bring the tripods
Or the artificial lights

It is not decadent to study decadence

I have a million close-ups to give you still
Is it creepy to turn oneself into feed?
Is it creepy to turn oneself into feed?
Or creepier to lie agape waiting to be fed by someone else

Heighten a breath of sorrow. Scream. ETC.

Their insides ripped off and sullied
Makes all imperative ghost allies into diamond dust
Something is sold on each line
To all CELESTIAL BEINGS in waves
in a cubby. Taken like a Morse code out of context
cubby up, with your chums, in a retreated patch
Take all her hair out of your notebook, breathe
Of each attempt to cut the throat of the enemy
Ready or not, he's still there
Sorry.
Be there for him as nurse
But don't be a cowering sniffle
NOW IN A VICTIM'S BREAKDOWN
SPEECH, burning up in hipster rubble
The heat all invented and then disappeared has nothing to do with
Your little hand. Pressed always on a crayon in a corner room. It's
Okay to be weary, fabricate your way up the ladder, then fabricate
Your way down

Bull NY Acad Med. 1939 Apr; 15(4): 258–266.

JB came for treatment at the age of twenty-five with depersonalization
symptoms which had existed for two years. He was good looking
and of superior musical talent. As so often occurs, the symptoms had
suddenly started during an episode of petting in which he had felt that
he had lost himself and his emotions. His sexual feelings also vanished
suddenly. This episode had followed an incomplete and disappointing
love affair with her employer. The final rejection by him had revived
the humiliations he had experienced in early childhood from his
father. The psychological treatment led to a recovery after two years.
The symptoms disappeared completely; however, one year after the
treatment, the patient had not yet made a sexual adaptation.

EI came for treatment at the age of twenty-one. Depersonalization
symptoms had persisted for several years. She complained "that things
were moving up and down before her eyes." "I feel my head is empty.
There is only a blank inside.... It is as if I would be asleep all the time. I
do not realize how time passes. My whole intelligence and personality
have disappeared. I have no desires anymore. I might as well be dead....
My voice has changed completely. Sensations are present but they do
not reach my head." The patient had also a wealth of hypochondriac
sensations, which pertained particularly to her abdomen. She was very
much concerned about her anal functions. A great hostility concerning
the mother reached back into early childhood. There were very lively
sadomasochistic phantasies since the age of five. The patient was
treated with group psychotherapy and lost almost all her symptoms;
however, in this case, also, no sexual adaptation was reached.

FB, twenty-three years old, came to treatment complaining he was
on a "never ending cannabis high." From an artist's family, he had
fond memories of being treated like a special erotic toy in shows and

games with his sister. After her suicide, he had abandonment fears and a sadomasochistic compulsion to exhibit and control his anus. He would use his symptoms of depersonalization to inspire sexually perverse art and emotionally overwrought poetry that was highly rewarded within his arts community. Because he was attempting to "profit" from disassociation, he would not seek treatment, until, after smoking cannabis, he found himself unable to access his traumatic sexual fantasies in a way that was productive to his art practice. In the name of "criticism," he became misanthropic and hostile towards other artists. It was only when he found he could not write any longer that he sought treatment. On October 4th, metrazol treatment was instituted. He received 4 1/2 grains intravenously and had no convulsion. From then on, up to the seventh of November, fifteen convulsions were produced; the first four with injections of 6 grains, the subsequent three with 7 grains, and the last eight with 9 grains. There were no particular incidents during the treatment. The improvement started after the third convulsion and progressed steadily. The clinical symptoms had practically disappeared after the tenth injection. The patient was discharged fully recovered and with full insight, but he still receives psychotherapeutic help.

EBB, thirty-one years old, comes from a family in which the father and one aunt had severe psychotic states probably of manic depressive character. She was always considered an outgoing personality. Also her brothers and sisters were energetic and successful. She was the oldest of five children, three girls and two boys. She had two children, one of whom was only a few months old when the patient got sick. The family was at that time in straitened financial circumstances. The illness started five months before admission to Bellevue Hospital. She complained that she always felt too tired and was disinclined to sexual intercourse. She ate very little and claimed that she had lost her sense of taste. She thought this was as a result of a cold. She became untidy in appearance and was preoccupied with the care of her children. She complained that she had lost interest in things; that she didn't belong to this world and that she couldn't cry. She was sent to a sanitarium. There she stated that she was not alive but had turned to stone and had no feelings and no emotions. In the sanitarium she swallowed several needles with suicidal intent, and was, therefore, sent to Bellevue Hospital, on September 10. She said: "I can't live, I don't feel at all, I just got fear of life, everything became complicated, everything turned in me, the whole world just looks flat. Nobody can help me. It feels as if I had no place on earth; nothing in the world belongs to me; I don't feel that my family and children belong to me; life has been taken out of me; I seem to be inside out. Everything looks backward; the heart doesn't seem to be in the same place; I can't change; just like a chair over there. It is as if the eyes would look inside instead of out. Time neither passes nor stands still. It doesn't seem like another day; there is no penetration of enjoyment. My mind goes round and round all the time in circles; the whole world looks flat to me. I know what torture you and everyone else is going through but no torture is greater than my misery." On the ward she was seclusive and did not talk spontaneously. However, she was very productive when one talked with her.

Lizzie

Lizzie Borden serves as a cautionary tale that is worthwhile for the middle school curriculum. Incorporate the precautions into your home.

The child raises his hand and when called on says: "My dad was a softie. I want it hard. Tho. as a supplement."

Sexual property of a girl of
Sexual (1823–1863) instincts
With that reality she remained
A Jew of high settings and her
Public caché to the schoolbooks
And the history and scientific
Schoolbooks, which never lie
And gave voice to her torturous
Conditions, mind clicking his boots
Away, tata tata tata, and they all
Joined in the ritual fun, it's
Enigmatic abuse and homicide
Or matricide or genocide, it's
Enigma. It's an erotic lesbian tale
Penned by Otto Frank.
Ritual abuse cults/groups can be both intergenerational and extra-familial
Perpetrators engage in organized efforts to discount the survivor's disclosure of their ritual abuse-torture ordeals

> <and from the trauma of being fed pot brownies by my sister at the age of 5>
> I don't like the implications of this no matter your reasoning. Change to brother.

also too much on the oedipal stuff, not because I am figured but I wouldn't recommend you figure yourself so much in that way—people will anyway, you will anyway. Let them but don't do do it to yourself, even as psychodrama satire.

Emma	Gabe	Cole	Susan
heart sunk	cut off from	brisk breeze	methodological
shot her pistil	mirages	mumble	discarded premises
grassy dew	sliding	wave plash	murky remains
maneuvered	abandonment	nor noise bent	tusks tumors
land unfolded	strawman	bumbling curve	veins temples
vacant port	turvy	strange crimpled	wasteland
peach	macaroni	radish	sauerkraut

Tata...Tata...   We're sick of (from) hearing about Auschwitz
Tata...Tata...   We're sick of (from) hearing about Auschwitz

In the Lizzie Borden poem the father always gets one more whack.

Conversation with EI

"The goal of these drawn and colored
Figures was to exorcise the curse, to vituperate
     Bodily against the exigencies of spatial form
Of perspective, of measure, of equilibrium,
     Of dimension and, via this vituperative act of
Protest to condemn the psychic world which,
     Like a crab louse, digs its way into the physical
And, like an incubus or succubus, claims to have
     Given it shape...
And the figures that I thereby made
     Were spells—which, after so meticulously
Having drawn, I put a match to."
     —Artaud

EI: I'm holding a mask with black lace pulled over the face lying in a bed of colored roses. My stare is cold.

FB: Are you a gifted child or the gift?

EI: I'm gifted with a little of the father's language, but I'm also the mother's gift, or at least her phallus, what she uses to navigate the patriarchal world. Mother dresses me in various costumes to help me assimilate as her surrogate—the better the clothing, the wealthier the child.

FB: But what happens when she undresses or unwraps the gifted child? You are always dressed as a "little rich women" but what class are you when undressed? Is that nudity or another costume?
EI: That's our dilemma, silly! We can never be nude, or exist for

ourselves. The father and mother make a kind of zygote that we must carry around inside and be full and sick on.

FB: Why do people play dead? Are you passive aggressive or aggressively passive?

EI: Passive aggression is very American (where the women passive aggressively eat donuts at home and get fat) and aggressive passivity is very French (where they starve into sexiness, too "passive to eat"). But I might be outside the passive aggressive spectrum completely...

FB: When I look at you, I think about Marlene Dietrich singing "Illusions," bitter and world-weary, even as a child; the little princess, who is pissed about the "pea," which she can feel always in her bed... You just decapitated someone in this photo. Who did you decapitate?

EI: The father/analyst/viewer. I have nothing to learn or adjust to, not even clothes.

FB: Here you look like a meal, spread on the dining room table, you do wear some clothes—a hat, a shawl, and pearls, but your nipples are still bare. It is not that you have a lack of clothes to wear....

EI: Remember, Felix, that Aphrodite wants to be with Adonis, her female version (you want this too...) but instead she gets married off to the ugly deformed Hephaestus, who gives her a lot of jewelry, but she doesn't like it.... You won't have to, or maybe you already have...

FB: "In April 2011, Eva's lawyer arranged for a seizure at the home of Irina Ionesco of a box of negatives labeled 'Eva.' In a judgment of December 17, 2012, the Paris trial court ruled that the seizure was not lawful, because it violated Irina Ionesco's property rights to her negatives." Negatives are interesting because they are the source from which reproduction can occur. Aphrodite is the goddess of procreation: an endless source. "Normally, intellectual property concerns creations. But a person does not create herself, apart from her style and appearance. What is personality and what is a person?" What is the daughter and what is the mother? When does the daughter become her own property?

EI: A person is the subject who is haunted...Poetry and social media is the mean parent, who demands that you give over your soul, emotions, and self on a daily basis, which you do, forgetting that you aren't just giving, you are also designing/constructing, as you give, to meet her appetite. What did you mean to capture when you used to photograph yourself nude? You know when you were a preteen...

FB: I guess I was trying to capture a fleeting moment of erotic adolescent sublime, and it could not be enjoyed because I was already trying so desperately to milk it and re-present it, that it could never be mine—that I did not own my own nude image; the state did, since I was always already child pornography, doomed to be confiscated.

EI: Note that I am always dressed as property in the pictures—as jewelry, a feast, and another ornament in the den.

FB: But you are always pouty and defiant, were you asked to do that; as a form of titillation?

EI: I was and wasn't asked—you see the object that resists is always anyways the child. I suppose the subject that resists is the father and the subject that accepts is the mother. I don't know what the object that accepts would be—a dead child?

FB: Why'd you attempt to legally seize your mother's negatives of you?

EI: To get rid of the positives—the joys—that was always the most unbearable part, because they were unavoidably pleasurable, despite being truly horrible and unlawful. How do you feel looking at me?

FB: Like Little Jack Horner, cornered into my shame with the pie—I guess I'm reminded of childhood's many forced enjoyments, which like you say, are horrible and unlawful. Can you ever burn the negatives? Or at least hide them in the attic?

EI: No, because pornographic, like the attic, is a façade—only threatening in so far as it signifies what's "beneath," which it signifies through a peek-a-boo dialectic of hiding and exposing. What you can do, though, is recognize that what is unlawful is also abysmal, but the abysmal is just a feeling, that you can *eventually* move through.

FB: Sadly, the images always end up belonging to the photographer, anyway. All one can do is get so much plastic surgery that it is no longer an image of yourself.

EI: "The copyright office says it takes no issue with naked images and a visual arts specialist at the office went so far as to recommend not redacting the photos and just sending the photos as is to make for a stronger copyright infringement case." Of course, the copyright office has no problem receiving naked pictures.

FB: "Experts, who have seen a rise in revenge porn, say the best bet for victims may be to copyright your body parts." "CNN recently reported about a woman who said she was forced to copyright her breasts after her long-distance ex-boyfriend posted her nude photos online to humiliate her."

EI: At what point can you protect yourself—after you've copyrighted yourself, that is already to forsake your body to the state—so either you copyright yourself and give yourself over to the state (who is happy to receive your nude pictures and stamp them, and this is perfectly legal) or you let the pictures be illicitly out there in the lawless world of the web.

FB: You have to be your own photographer to be safe. Maybe that is also how you and I protected ourselves; by imagining ourselves to be in control—as the stager and the staged.

EI: And as the stage itself...

FB: I admire how you do not express happiness.

EI: I think it is scarier for a little girl to show it than for a boy. Even though I wasn't ashamed of being nude, I was ashamed of happiness.

FB: I was ashamed of nudity but not happiness... But then my happiness was also my weakness, my gullibility, my eagerness to be fed cake, and not merely "enjoy" it but subversively and self-critically enjoy it...More Sadean than Kantian. In the sense, that my sister was Sade.

EI: Maybe she was just looking for a source of autonomous pleasure?

FB: Or trying to taunt *the* source of pleasure, the "viewer," to get him to pay attention to problems that were unrelated to the masquerade... problems that she didn't even know.

EI: I'm wearing a white sparkly shirt, in this one, my hair is very long, and I'm standing on tiptoes, leaning in for a kiss from mother. You can't see my eyes so you don't know if they are angry, my mother's hands are holding mine, I don't even remember how I felt then...

FB: It looks as though you are reaching up but your mother isn't leaning down...

EI: She's evil but her love looks so valuable.

FB: Is it? To me she looks greedy and grubby like the mother in *Flowers in the Attic*. You have a ring on your ring finger.... Were you fantasizing escape?

EI: No union.

FB: Maybe both?

EI: It's the moth to a flame conundrum—if the moth has union with the flame it will die in flames, but if it goes too far out of its orbit it loses heat and light.

FB: We're so desperately trying to preserve the right distance between burning up and losing all heat.

EI: And this is why we can never burn the negatives, no matter how abysmal, not really, not ever really...

Sexy

A well-developed 14-year-old spends her summer vacation trying to figure out whether and with whom to get laid. Boys or men?

Ten-year-old Harriet runs a rustic motel with her alcoholic mom and her slutty big sister, Gwen. She dreams of escape—either alien abduction or balloon-propelled lawnchair.

Fourteen-year-old Ellie Christianson wants to make her father Ben her love partner. And when her mother Karen turns up dead, Ellie has a good opportunity.

A look at the work and surprising success of a four-year-old girl whose paintings have been compared to the likes of Picasso and have raked in hundreds of thousands of dollars.

In 1929 French Indochina, a French teenage girl embarks on a reckless and forbidden romance with a wealthy, older Chinese man, each knowing that knowledge of their affair will bring drastic consequences to the other.

A look inside an offbeat boarding school for young girls.

A wealthy author's second wife begins to suspect her 12-year-old stepson may have murdered his mother, who mysteriously died in a bathtub accident.

A drama set in the American South, where a precocious, troubled girl finds a safe haven in the music and movement of Elvis Presley.

The life of a boy in the streets of Sao Paulo, involved with little crimes, prostitution, etc.

Two precocious boys explore their sexuality at boarding school.

A journalist becomes the unwanted center of attention for a 14-year-old girl whom proceeds to sabotage his life after he refuses her sexual advances.

Lorenzo, a handsome first-year professor in an isolated Italian village, falls under the spell of his most beguiling pupil.

A 13-year-old girl's relationship with her mother is put to the test as she discovers drugs, sex, and petty crime in the company of her cool but troubled best friend.

During the Great Depression, a con man finds himself saddled with a young girl who may or may not be his daughter, and the two forge an unlikely partnership.

A 10-year-old girl named Angela leads her 6-year-old sister Ellie through various regimens of purification.

Mondo is a homeless young boy, with a big smile, who wanders around Nice looking for food and a place to sleep.

In the Victorian period, two children are shipwrecked on a tropical island in the South Pacific. With no adults to guide them, the two make a simple life together, unaware that sexual maturity will eventually intervene.

After her mother dies, 14-year-old Marion falls in love with her stepfather Remy.

A man marries his landlady so he can take advantage of her daughter.

Ludovic is a small boy who cross-dresses and generally acts like a girl.

In Catholic and traditionalist Italy, two teen-agers covertly discover new prohibited games.

A high school student's love for a 15-year-old girl is thwarted by parental disapproval, circumstance, and accident.

Lester Burnham, a depressed suburban father in a mid-life crisis, decides to turn his hectic life around after developing an infatuation for his daughter's attractive friend.

Sculptor Paul meets a former great love again after a long time—but is much more impressed by her 15-year-old daughter Laura.

As a group of Danish children pass into adolescence, gradually the most popular girl becomes an outcast.

Suzanne is 15 and is having sex with many boys, just for fun, but does not manage to really love any of them.

A group of teenage summer campers and one counselor share the stories of their first sexual experiences when an avalanche traps them in a cave.

A rebellious Malibu princess is shipped off to a strict English boarding school by her father.

The story revolves around a 23-year-old grade school teacher named Daisuke Aoki whose main problem is that one of his students named Rin Kokonoe has a crush on him.

A group of teen boys go to Rome in this controversial art film. Confounded by clashes with the seemingly rule-obsessed world, the boys seek enlightenment from an unconventional drama teacher. First love, first sex, first self-made theatre performance of *Romeo and Juliet*.

Jacob is trapped in a Polish ghetto during the Second World War with thousands of other Jews facing starvation or deportation to death camps. One night he overhears a radio broadcast in Gestapo headquarters that says the Russians are only twenty kilometers away. He spreads the word and it gives hope to everyone in the ghetto. They ask him for more news and he pretends that he has access to a hidden radio. In his care is a charming 10-year-old orphan, Lina, a skinny pigtailed waif in a hand-me-down dress that's too small. He uses the fantasy of the radio to distract her from the harsh reality of their impending fate.

Eva is raised by her grandmother. Her mother Hannah tries to make a living on taking photographs and concentrates on her dreams to become a famous artist. In order to succeed as an artist she doesn't worry about dating men of questionable reputation. Only every now and then her mother visits her daughter but during these occasions it occurs to her that her daughter could be a potential model. She starts exploiting her daughter who by transforming into a kind of Lolita becomes increasingly alienated from other children of her age. At school she is frequently insulted and rejected. Then Mamie dies and Hannah's photographs are about to unequivocally overstep the line of acceptability. Hannah even coerces Eva mercilessly into cooperation by withholding her food in case she doesn't agree to pose for increasingly daring photographs.

Felix is a boy coming of age in Manhattan: he has overdetermined his life based on exaggerating trivial familial conflicts. He thinks about killing his mother and marrying his father during his therapy sessions paid for by his parents and he lives at home. He attempts to punctuate his transgressions. But each time he puts a period at the end of a sentence, he pacifies the grudge, and loses steam. And when the steam is all gone, he simply stops. And to not wear that glittery necklace of references which you can link arms with, to not be satanic,

seductive, or brilliant, to not kill your mother or yourself is to be alone
and ugly: kvetching in an unmarked puddle of spittle: curly haired and
precociously ambitious, climbing ladders then tossing them aside.

Once I was the passionate freak in the middle of the circle jerk waiting
to be sprayed. I was the homo transgressor. I was the heir to an
aesthetic fortune and I couldn't wait to suck it all up.

But then I chose not to kill my mom, not to marry my father, not to kill
myself, not to be confused or ambivalent, not to be negative or positive,
satanic or flamboyant.

Eva's sexy. Justin's sexy.
Sister's sexy. Gabe's sexy.
Ryan's sexy. Andrew's sexy.

But I'm not murderous, exploited, riddling, manic, suffering, or voided.

        I'm not sexy.

I'm just a striver—indifferent yet ambitious
frigidly waiting for the cum to spray my face
so I can smile and drip and pretend to care.

The only reason I'm here is out of fear, is to seek protection, from the inevitable hatred I will receive, from the generosity of my open-hearted understandings of this moment.

I can't decipher what I have left to say to my mother, it's her last day of work, before the strange occurrence happens on a micro-level, with which you can identify like a banner in the air (from afar I attract the eye of the marvelous lover to my enclosed world).

I got invited again, without recourse to friendship, some can consider what they do to be auto-deconstructive, casting pressure against their own hype, and having fun with the motions of spinning, that occur when seeking protection, gives out.

The disappearing act of what my work even is, as long as it is dismissed, by me first, then can be, like a received idea actually increases production, but I don't. I lie.

They play the game at a very high level, I am cautioned. And the poets and artists we all know are bad are excused because when you talk to them they really understand their own work. How much time do you have to understand yours? To know what your little errors are so that you can avoid them by not actually avoiding them, but by noticing them.

I can't decipher what I have I have left to say to my mother, it's her last day of work.

Softening the glance at the man's house and the way that it is also a site for reminding you of your own house and together that you can bond through sex and laughter about the fact of a shared commitment to not being racist. To not actually laughing. To having been gutted from the inside out but still desiring to stand up and talk.

In writing this to you I write under the assumption that...

Some days the dissolve is harder to take, but the human reality of it, being able to witness the cadres, and the fights: you know, I play old movies all the time to unconsciously absorb them in my system, I'm actually a 50s housewife, just like my mom, she suffered, and I do too, and I think suffering is beauty, third-generation repetition of the same remarks, etc. etc.

We can play this game together at a very high level, I mean the game of exclusion, excluding you from the beautiful room, and then you exclude me, even though I trusted Kafka was right ("the beautiful room is not empty") when my sister died and I still thought I was her replacement, and was the same thing for my mother she had been, but I was actually not the same thing, I was me.

The discovery of "I am me" should not startle you yet. The fact, that someone in the family is whimpering and nihilistic is not enough to startle me. If you want to startle me, you should probably attempt to say that there is some investment of beauty available to us in the kinship pattern, that relationships don't end every four years, and that by avoiding being a bad dad, you don't become a worse one.

What startles me about this, though, is the way in which you are able to bring the micro-conflict of the family unit into the light of day without...

Here I stop because I need you to fill in the rest for me. What I am is not able to fill in my own blanks, rub my own back, so that is where you come in, as an appendage to my sore back. Which is caused by my overreactions to your temperament. Always imagining that the room is emptier and colder than it actually is.

When I get you back, and I always do, because I am not a nihilist, I tend to think that the inclusion of the sap will be what really finally sticks you to me.

As long as the artist understands their art from all viewpoints, or is able to understand how regressive and stiflingly boring they are—then the artist is still golden.

I have a fairly good grasp of what game I played. When making this or making you appear to be disappearing because you were always there, i.e., those trips to Buffalo were just a virtual absence.

My heart is always full of you.

February 23, 2015

Not everything I do is good.
Need to remember how to make things me to me again or I'll burn out.
The absence of uncovery keeps me uncovering
But I'm sick of it. So I wait.
Just wait. No mystical renunciation or beautiful soliloquy or insider culture
or self-understanding. Maybe a mentor but a sordid one with ulterior
motives. No enjoyment of friendship or strong feelings for the earth.
Nobody lifts me on their back and gives me sustenance. Nor does the room
start being more than a room. No lift-off or open sesame. I can't make it go
boom or bam. No break from pornography, captive audiences everywhere.
No friend who isn't scheming to make something of me. No mixture
of sweet funny incidents. No right job or right family or chosen family.
Nobody remembers her except once a year. People only pretend to like
my parents. There is a trade-off that was made for me and now I look like
I'm reneging on it. No people getting along who aren't equally disgusting.
Nobody doesn't ignore that one artist but he comes to every party.
Everybody wants equally to be loved and felt up. I'm no different than the
other person who shows their dick. I don't want to think my ubiquitous
specialness makes me part of a community of Westerners but it does.
Nobody pricks me anymore, or tries to make me feel like a little kid. I'm
not afraid of the dark anymore. I'm not afraid to mention or impersonate
childhood anymore, even though it's not very experimental. I'll happily
listen to people talk about how much they want to kill themselves. Because
no amount of friendly advice changes fate. I'll tell myself that I am more
intelligent than a group of people that surround me, and I'll be right. Then
later I'll feel like an idiot. Then I'll think this is a rather trivial complex.
No explosion happens in my writing that gets rid of selfishness. Nobody
is a good writer to me anymore. I want pretty badly to have friends but

then I remember that this writing is about something else. I'm not meant to have more than this. But that gives me a kind of ghost friendship with other loners. I don't want that but I seem to have it anyway. When I think of myself as a loner I want to barf, when I think of myself as a performer, I want to barf. I have an online presence. Everyone with an online presence is morally bankrupt. Too many people have attempted to escape me. I have a grip only over a very small aspect of culture. But it will be enough to get me tenure. Was always worried that when I grew up I would not be able to fuck children anymore. It was true. Confession is always incredibly loveable.

Sui Cide

Glass child at looking glass
Glares at her own half grimace
Cloaked in a hollow tree in a
Beechwood forest she has no
Need for funereal longing or
Love poetry, shrouded, she
Sits in spidery light and
Stares, not desperate but
Light like a linnet, she
Dissolves into imago and
Sheds the salty shelling
That kept her wed to the
Misguided strangers, who
Sneak around her to get
A peek. Waves crash at
Her feet. And she
Sucks in all men from
Their masts then returns
To her soil and
Rots

Just take it from me
I'm just as free as
Any daughter
I do just what
I like
And how I
Love it

May she become a
Flourishing hidden
Tree, out by his
Bridge, she waits
And waits, drowns

Pagliaccio
Picks her
Up.

Felix Bernstein debuted on YouTube with his satirically real high-school coming-out video in 2008; going on to play Amy Winehouse, Leopold Brant, and Lamb Chop. Bernstein's writings have appeared in *BOMB, The Believer, Hyperallergic, The Awl,* and *Poetry Magazine.* His critical essays were collected in *Notes on Post-Conceptual Poetry.* He makes music and films with Gabe Rubin. His musical *Adonais or Bieber Bathos Elegy,* will premiere in January 2016 at the Whitney Museum of American Art.

ACKNOWLEDGEMENTS

Thanks to Cammisa Buerhaus, Cecilia Corrigan, Clara Lipfert, Cole Heinowitz, Frank Guan, Jay Sanders, Joyelle McSweeney, Lonely Christopher, Monroe Lawrence, Nada Gordon, Nellie Barber, Stephen Motika, Trisha Low, and Willie Gurner for offering inspiration and advice. Thanks to Cassie Seltman for writing the character Eva (E.I.).

Poems in this book have appeared in *Prelude* and *The Brooklyn Rail.*

Nightboat Books, a nonprofit organization, seeks to develop audiences for writers whose work resists convention and transcends boundaries. We publish books rich with poignancy, intelligence, and risk. Please visit our website, www.nightboat.org, to learn about our titles and how you can support our future publications.

The following individuals have supported the publication of this book. We thank them for their generosity and commitment to the mission of Nightboat Books:

Elizabeth Motika
Benjamin Taylor

In addition, this book has been made possible, in part, by grants from the National Endowment for the Arts and the New York State Council on the Arts Literature Program.